The Critical Idiom
General Editor: JOHN D. JUMP

30 The Ode

In the same series

The Ode/*John D. Jump*

Methuen & Co Ltd

First published 1974
by Methuen & Co Ltd
11 New Fetter Lane London EC4P 4EE
© *1974 John D. Jump*
Printed in Great Britain by
Cox & Wyman Ltd, Fakenham, Norfolk

SBN   416 78810 6   Hardback
SBN   416 78820 3   Paperback

Distributed in the U.S.A. by

HARPER & ROW PUBLISHERS, INC.
BARNES & NOBLE IMPORT DIVISION

To BARBARA *and* KATE

Contents

Contents

General Editor's Preface

The volumes composing the Critical Idiom deal with a wide variety of key terms in our critical vocabulary. The purpose of the series differs from that served by the standard glossaries of literary terms. Many terms are adequately defined for the needs of students by the brief entries in these glossaries, and such terms do not call for attention in the present series. But there are other terms which cannot be made familiar by means of compact definitions. Students need to grow accustomed to them through simple and straightforward but reasonably full discussions. The main purpose of this series is to provide such discussions.

Many critics have borrowed methods and criteria from currently influential bodies of knowledge or belief that have developed without particular reference to literature. In our own century, some of them have drawn on art-history, psychology, or sociology. Others, strong in a comprehensive faith, have looked at literature and literary criticism from a Marxist or a Christian or some other sharply defined point of view. The result has been the importation into literary criticism of terms from the vocabularies of these sciences and creeds. Discussions of such bodies of knowledge and belief in their bearing upon literature and literary criticism form a natural extension of the initial aim of the Critical Idiom.

Because of their diversity of subject-matter, the studies in the series vary considerably in structure. But all authors have tried to give as full illustrative quotation as possible, to make reference whenever appropriate to more than one literature, and to write in such a way as to guide readers towards the short bibliographies in which they have made suggestions for further reading.

John D. Jump

University of Manchester

I

Classical Models

In the long, extravagant, and highly entertaining scene that
dominates Act IV of *Love's Labour's Lost*, an eavesdropper
spies on an eavesdropper who spies on an eavesdropper who
spies on Dumaine. All four have broken a solemn if absurd vow
by falling in love, and the perfidy of each soon becomes known to
all. Dumaine, entering last, is overheard by the other three when
he sighs out his love for Katharine and says, 'Once more Ile read
the Ode that I haue writ' (IV. iii. 97). He proceeds to do so.

His 'Ode' turns out to be a short love-lyric giving fanciful
expression to his personal predicament. It is quite unlike anything
that we should incline to call an ode today. Shakespeare uses the
word on one other occasion. In *As You Like It*, III. ii. 352–5,
the disguised Rosalind teases the love-sick Orlando by saying,
'There is a man haunts the Forrest, that abuses our yong plants
with caruing *Rosalinde* on their barkes; hangs Oades vpon
Hauthornes, and Elegies on brambles; all (forsooth) de[i]fying
the name of *Rosalinde.*' These 'Oades', too, are slighter things
than the title would now lead us to expect.

If a twentieth-century English reader were asked to name a
few odes, Andrew Marvell's 'Horatian Ode upon Cromwel's
Return from Ireland', William Wordsworth's 'Ode: Intimations
of Immortality from Recollections of Early Childhood', and
John Keats's 'Ode to a Nightingale' would probably come early
in his list. These are all longer and weightier poems than Dumaine
and Rosalind have in mind; they are reflective, philosophical,
descriptive.

Epithets such as these would be too much for the modest piece of verse that was the first in English to be dignified by the label, 'Ode'. In 1582, Thomas Watson, a minor poet who later became a friend of Christopher Marlowe, published his Ἑκατομπαθία. He does not call any of his poems odes, though he does introduce the term several times in his explanatory notes; but a commendatory poem which a friend prefixed to his collection carries the title 'An Ode, written to the Muses Concerning this Authour'. It is short: eighteen iambic pentameters, rhymed as three sestets each consisting of a quatrain followed by a couplet. It takes the form of an earnest invitation to the Muses, the 'sacred *Nymphes, Apolloes* sisters faire', to reside in Britain as Watson's guests. In theme, form, and manner, it is closer to the ode as we now understand it than are the poems of which Dumaine and Rosalind were to speak in the following decade.

But the phrase 'the ode as we understand it' covers a wide area of divergent and conflicting opinions. With exemplary honesty, the *Oxford Dictionary* reflects these in its definition: 'A rimed (rarely unrimed) lyric, often in the form of an address; generally dignified or exalted in subject, feeling, and style, but sometimes (in earlier use) simple and familiar (though less so than a *song*)'. Here the adverbs, 'often', 'generally', and 'sometimes', and the first and last of the three parentheses, serve to blur a definition that would be unacceptable if it were sharp.

A swift review of a few other attempts at definition will further illustrate the difficulties. Edmund Gosse takes as an ode 'any strain of enthusiastic and exalted lyrical verse, directed to a fixed purpose, and dealing progressively with one dignified theme'; William Sharp suggests 'that any poem finely wrought, and full of high thinking, which is of the nature of an apostrophe, or of sustained intellectual meditation on a single theme of general purport, should be classed as an ode'; Robert Shafer, who quotes both of these in his *English Ode to 1660*, requires 'that a true ode be a lyrical poem, serious in tone and stately in its structure; that it be cast in the form of an address; that it be rapid in style, treating its subject with "brevity and variety"; and that its unity be emotional in character' (p. 3); and George N. Shuster, after quoting further attempts in his *English Ode from Milton to Keats*, declares that the 'element of address is of no especial significance, being merely a reflection of the classical influence', and for the purposes of his treatise takes an ode to be 'a lyric poem derived, either directly or indirectly, from Pindaric models' (pp. 11–12).

This last phrase offers us a useful clue. Many English odes belong to a tradition stemming from the work of the Classical Greek poet, Pindar, and many others belong to a tradition stemming from that of the Classical Latin poet, Horace. The two traditions can mingle, Horace himself having become something of a Pindarist. From the Romantic period onwards, we lose sight of each for long stretches; but, before that period, if they are often inseparable they are rarely indistinguishable.

Shuster would add two other great exemplars: the Greek, Anacreon; and King David the Psalmist. Anacreon's influence has been considerable, but it appears in songs and short lyrics rather than in odes; and, while the Psalmist has provided a pervasive inspiration throughout much of our literature, he has not influenced the actual form of our odes. Pindar and Horace remain for our purposes the two dominant figures. By examining the tradition descending from each, we shall be helping ourselves to a clearer understanding of the range and variety of poetic achievement possible in the ode. We must start with Pindar and Horace themselves.

PINDAR

In the seventh and sixth centuries before Christ, Greek lyrics, or poems to be sung to the lyre, took two forms. There were monodies, sung by single persons, and choral odes, sung by choirs.

If we may judge by the fragments in which their works have come down to us, Alcaeus and Sappho were among the finest monodists. But our main concern is with the choral odes.

These had originated in religious celebrations and were performed at festivals and on other important occasions, human and divine. They normally included four elements: prayers or praise to the gods, stories or myths from the heroic past, moral maxims, and personal references appropriate to the circumstances of the performance. Their tone was grave and dignified.

Naturally, they developed differently in the hands of different poets. Though the extant writings of Alcman and Stesichorus are tantalizingly fragmentary, critics have felt able to speak of the freshness and charm of the former and the heroic temper of the latter. To a third poet, Simonides, is ascribed the shaping of the epinician ode, the choral song in honour of a victory in the Olympic or other games. This was to find its greatest exponent in Pindar (518 B.C.–c. 438 B.C.).

The games are little more than Pindar's point of departure. From them he invariably proceeds with little or no delay to matters of wider scope and deeper significance. Men win in the games, he believes, because they have natural talent, develop it by hard toil, and enjoy the favour of the gods. Life everywhere owes its splendour to just such high endeavour as they manifest. Their successes bring them exhilaration and exaltation, an extension and enrichment of consciousness, a dazzling glory, and a sort of immortality in the memory of an admiring posterity.

> For if any man delights in expense and effort
> And sets in action high gifts shaped by the Gods,
> And with him his destiny
> Plants the glory which he desires,
> Already he casts his anchor on the furthest edge of bliss,
> And the Gods honour him.
>
> ('Isthmian VI': trans. Bowra)

Seeing this significance in sporting triumphs, Pindar is a deeply religious poet.

The restriction of his immediate subject-matter does not prevent him from displaying considerable enterprise and boldness in his handling of details. He introduces myths which he has chosen for their relevance to his themes or patrons or both. He handles these myths briefly and allusively, often leaving his reader or hearer to supply links between the topics on which he touches and to guess intentions which he does not declare. His boldness and swiftness show, too, in his syntax and in his choice of words. But he always works within regular metrical and stanzaic limits. Thirty-eight of his forty-four epinician odes are written in triads. Each triad consists of three stanzas: strophe, antistrophe, and epode. In any single ode, all the strophes and antistrophes have one and the same metrical form. The metrical form of the epodes differs from this, but it remains the same for all the epodes in the poem. The triadic form, said to have been invented by Stesichorus, was a favourite not only with Pindar but also with his contemporary and rival, Bacchylides. It relates to the dancing which accompanied the singing of an ode; during the strophe and antistrophe the chorus would be in movement, while during the epode it would be at rest.

Pindar was both a painstaking craftsman and an ardent believer in the need for inspiration. The Greeks felt that he sometimes failed to maintain the elevation and magnificence of his best writing. But this did not prevent them from considering him their greatest lyric poet.

HORACE

Horace (Quintus Horatius Flaccus, 65 B.C.–8 B.C.) lived four hundred and fifty years later, at a time when a monarchical order was displacing the old republican order in Rome. He served as an officer in the republican army that suffered defeat at Philippi and has left in one of his odes a cheerfully self-depreciatory allusion to his jettisoning his shield in the flight. Before long he made his peace with the new authorities, and through his patron and friend Maecenas he became favourably known to Augustus himself.

Horace was no fanatic. He enjoyed a quiet life and practised a moderate, though quite unspeculative, Epicureanism. He was a keen observer, and in his poetry he raised worldly common sense to the level of wisdom. In his *Satires*, he does what Ben Jonson was later to profess to do, that is, he sports with human follies, not with crimes. He is equally cool and poised in his *Epistles*, easy and elegant poems of manners and society.

Some of the characteristic qualities of his *Odes* may be suggested to readers who have little Latin by the example of a poem which John Milton translated into English. In this, Horace addresses the inconstant Pyrrha, whose latest lover fondly hopes that she will remain always free and amiable. In fact, she will change as completely as the sea changes when dark winds bring storms. Horace pities those to whom she still seems fair. He has himself narrowly escaped drowning, and a votive tablet on the temple wall shows that he has hung up his wet garments as an offering to Neptune.

> Quis multa gracilis te puer in rosa
> Perfusus liquidis urget odoribus
>   Grato, Pyrrha, sub antro?
>   Cui flavam religas comam,
>
> Simplex munditiis? heu quotiens fidem
> Mutatosque deos flebit et aspera
>   Nigris aequora ventis
>   Emirabitur insolens,
>
> Qui nunc te fruitur credulus aurea,
> Qui semper vacuam, semper amabilem
>   Sperat, nescius aurae
>   Fallacis. Miseri, quibus

Intemptata nites. Me tabula sacer
Votiva paries indicat uvida
   Suspendisse potenti
   Vestimenta maris deo.

                          (*Odes*, I. v)

In Milton's version, this ode is '*Rendred almost word for word without Rhyme according to the Latin Measure, as near as the Language will permit*'.

> What slender Youth bedew'd with liquid odours
> Courts thee on Roses in some pleasant Cave,
>   *Pyrrha* for whom bind'st thou
>   In wreaths thy golden Hair,
> Plain in thy neatness; O how oft shall he
> On Faith and changed Gods complain: and Seas
>   Rough with black winds and storms
>   Unwonted shall admire:
> Who now enjoyes thee credulous, all Gold,
> Who alwayes vacant, always amiable
>   Hopes thee; of flattering gales
>   Unmindfull. Hapless they
> To whom thou untry'd seem'st fair. Me in my vow'd
> Picture the sacred wall declares t' have hung
>   My dank and dropping weeds
>   To the stern God of Sea.

This is very far from colloquial English. But its latinate syntax and word-order give it a compactness and a resiliency which could hardly have been attained in a more relaxed idiom. Admittedly, it has lost the ease of expression that Horace invariably preserves within his strict formal limits. But Milton's final lines keep the note of gentle self-mockery with which Horace speaks of dedicating his wet clothes to the powerful god of the sea. It would be hard to find a more faithful rendering in English of the movement of thought, the feeling, and the tone of an Horatian ode.

B

The poem should not be read as a personal confession. Pyrrha
is merely the starting-point. What evidently interests Horace is
the parallel he can draw between the sufferings which await a
lover and those which await a traveller by sea, sufferings which
can be catastrophic but which have also their comic side.

Elsewhere a similarly urbane irony plays upon quite explicit
moralizing. He opens *Odes* I. xxii by declaring that a man 'Integer
vitae scelerisque purus' ('Of upright life and unstained by crimes')
has nothing in the world to fear. But he illustrates this maxim with
a piece of extravagant autobiography. He alleges that one day
while he was wandering unarmed near his Sabine farm singing of
Lalage, he met a ferocious wolf which astonishingly fled from him.
Inferring that his love for Lalage has saved him, he declares that
in all future trials and perils,

> Dulce ridentem Lalagen amabo,
> Dulce loquentem.
> ('I shall love the sweetly-smiling, sweetly-chattering Lalage.')

This surprise ending with its blithe false logic reflects ironically
upon the apparently solemn beginning. But Horace is never
really solemn. Though he wishes us to take his views seriously, he
declines to make heavy weather of them. Even when Octavian,
the future Emperor Augustus, succeeded in interesting him in his
political aims and ideals, Horace expressed his sincere concern
with a flexibility and a poise that distinguish him sharply from
any ordinary downright polemicist. Political themes remain
subordinate to personal themes in the earlier books of the *Odes*.
But in the famous 'Roman' odes at the beginning of the third
book, and in the odes of the fourth and last book, written fifteen
years later, Horace reveals himself as more fully committed to the
imperial régime which has successfully restored order after
generations of war and civil war. Correspondingly, the odes
acquire a severer formality. The spirit of Pindar becomes more

influential, whereas Alcaeus and Sappho prevailed in the earlier books.

Gilbert Highet in *The Classical Tradition* distinguishes clearly between the Pindaric and Horatian traditions in Western literature:

> The Pindarics admire passion, daring, and extravagance. Horace's followers prefer reflection, moderation, economy. Pindaric odes follow no pre-established routine, but soar and dive and veer as the wind catches their wing. Horatian lyrics work on quiet, short, well-balanced systems. Pindar represents the ideals of aristocracy, careless courage and the generous heart. Horace is a *bourgeois*, prizing thrift, care, caution, the virtue of self-control. Even the music we can hear through the odes of the two poets and their successors is different. Pindar loves the choir, the festival, and the many-footed dance. Horace is a solo singer, sitting in a pleasant room or quiet garden with his lyre.
>
> Characteristically, Horace often undervalued his own poems. Brief, orderly, tranquil, meditative, they are less intense and rhapsodical but deeper and more memorable than those of Pindar. Cool but moving, sensitive but controlled, elusive but profound, they contain more phrases of unforgettable eloquence and wisdom than any other group of lyrics in European literature.

(pp. 226–7)

2
Pindaric Odes

Shakespeare's use of the word 'ode' was normal enough in his time and place. Pierre de Ronsard (1524–85), the leading figure in the French group known as the 'Pléiade', had so labelled poems of his own that differed widely from one another in form and in substance. They ranged from a number of miniature pieces, or 'odelettes', written on the model of Anacreon, to fifteen elaborate Pindaric odes, the longest being an 816-line giant addressed to Ronsard's protector, Michel de l'Hospital. Following Ronsard's lead, the English poets of the fifteen-nineties felt free to give the name to almost any sort of lyric.

The first Englishman to claim to have written a Pindaric ode was apparently a poetaster named John Soothern in a volume published in 1584. He certainly plundered the Pindarics of Ronsard, but nothing in his three odes and three 'Odellets' suggests that he knew those of the Greek himself. Indeed, Pindar aroused very little interest in England during the sixteenth century, despite the fact that contemporary Continental interest was lively enough to call for the publication of a whole series of printed editions. The earliest English edition was to appear only at the end of the following century, in 1697.

In a poetical miscellany issued in 1602, the word 'ode' acquires a slightly more definite meaning, being reserved mainly for poems written in complex stanza forms. But Michael Drayton (1563–1631) recognized that the Classical odes had been distinctive in substance as well as in form. In a prose address to his readers he briefly characterizes the transcendently lofty odes of Pindar, the soft and amorous lyrics of Anacreon, and the odes of a mixed kind written by Horace. Nineteen of his own, printed in 1606 and 1619, vary appreciably from one another. Anacreon's influence upon them extends further than the poem in which it is announced, 'An Amouret Anacreontick'; and Horace's pervades almost the entire corpus. But Drayton owes much also to the English tradition. By fusing native and Classical elements – in 'To the Virginian Voyage' and 'His Ballad of Agincourt', for example – he reflects on a smaller scale the important achievement of the English Renaissance playwrights.

On Christmas Day, 1629, John Milton (1608–74) began his great ode 'On the Morning of Christs Nativity'. Though he is known to have studied Pindar closely, Milton did not use the triadic form which Pindar favoured but a monostrophic form such as the Greek had occasionally employed. Four stanzas written in a variant of rime royal introduce the 'Hymn' or 'humble ode' written in twenty-seven stanzas of a type apparently devised by Milton himself. All stanzas, both in 'The Hymn' and in the introduction, end with alexandrines, perhaps under the influence of Milton's 'sage and serious' master, Edmund Spenser. In 'The Hymn' itself, the shifting between shorter and longer lines, with the longer prevailing as each stanza draws to its close, leads up repeatedly to concluding alexandrines of impressive amplitude and weight:

> Ring out ye Crystall sphears,
> Once bless our human ears,
>   (If ye have power to touch our senses so)
> And let your silver chime
> Move in melodious time;
>   And let the Base of Heav'ns deep Organ blow,
> And with your ninefold harmony
> Make up full consort to th' Angelike symphony.

In a number of ways the poem reminds us of Pindar. Its rich language and striking imagery, its oblique allusions and swift transitions, and its impassioned lyricism and transcendent loftiness are all characteristics that it shares with the triumphal odes of the Greek.

Similar qualities characterize the Pindaric ode 'To the immortall memorie, and friendship of that noble paire, Sir Lucius Cary and Sir H. Morison', which Ben Jonson (?1573–1637) wrote about the same time. Jonson contrasts the brief existence which enabled Henry Morison to prove himself an active and worthy soldier, patriot, friend, and son, with the longer career of an unnamed man who after a promising start 'did no good' for the last sixty of his eighty years. Virtuous achievement, not mere duration, gives value to life. Turning to Lucius Cary, the young friend who has outlived Morison, Jonson assures him that the dead man, having 'leap'd the present age', survives in eternity; and that fate, having separated the pair, 'doth so alternate the designe' that while one of them now shines in heaven, the other still brightens the earth

The Turne

It is not growing like a tree
In bulke, doth make man better bee;
Or standing long an Oake, three hundred yeare,
To fall a logge at last, dry, bald, and seare:
A Lillie of a Day,
Is fairer farre, in May,
Although it fall, and die that night;
It was the Plant, and flowre of light.
In small proportions, we just beauties see:
And in short measures, life may perfect bee.

The Counter-turne

Call, noble *Lucius*, then for Wine,
And let thy lookes with gladnesse shine:
Accept this garland, plant it on thy head,

And thinke, nay know, thy *Morison*'s not dead.
He leap'd the present age,
Possest with holy rage,
To see that bright eternall Day:
Of which we *Priests*, and *Poëts* say
Such truths, as we expect for happy men,
And there he lives with memorie; and *Ben*

The Stand

Jonson, who sung this of him, e're he went
Himselfe to rest,
Or taste a part of that full joy he meant
To have exprest,
In this bright *Asterisme*:
Where it were friendships schisme,
(Were not his *Lucius* long with us to tarry)
To separate these twi-
Lights, the *Dioscuri*;
And keepe the one halfe from his *Harry*.
But fate doth so alternate the design,
Whilst that in heav'n, this light on earth must shine.

This is the third of the four triads that make up the poem.
Jonson has given English names to the strophe, antistrophe, and
epode: 'The Turne', 'The Counter-turne', and 'The Stand'. The
metrical form and rhyme-scheme of the turn are identical with
those of the counter-turn, and with those of all the other turns and
counter-turns in the poem; the metrical form and rhyme-scheme
of the stand differ from these but are identical with those of all
the other stands in the poem, apart from a slight variation at the
beginning of the second. Since the principles governing Greek
metres differed from those governing English metres, and since
Greek poetry made no use of rhyme, what Jonson offers is not an
exact reproduction of what we meet in Pindar. But it is as close
an equivalent as the nature of the two languages and poetic
traditions allows.

He had precedents in Pindar for letting the sense of the counter-turn or antistrophe in the passage just quoted run uninterruptedly into the stand or epode. But his discipleship to Pindar goes further than this. It appears in the bold imagery, and especially the imagery of light and brightness; in the passing reference to the myth of the Dioscuri, Castor and Polydeuces; in the introduction into the poem of the panegyrist, Ben Jonson, himself; in the weighty moral maxims; in the rapid transitions from topic to topic; and in the deliberately lofty tone. Jonson, however, is the cooler, the less impassioned of the two. We are not surprised to find that in general his odes are more Horatian than Pindaric. Nevertheless, in the example that has concerned us here we have the first close approximation in English to the characteristic achievement of Pindar. Nothing else as close as this was to appear during the seventeenth century.

LAX AND LAWLESS VERSIFICATION

In the middle of that century Abraham Cowley (1618–67) tried to reproduce Pindar's spirit and manner without imitating his metrical and stanzaic forms. According to Thomas Sprat (1635–1713), the historian of the Royal Society, 'The occasion of his falling on the Pindaric way of Writing was his accidental meeting with *Pindars* Works in a place where he had no other Books to direct him. Having then considered at leisure the height of his Invention and the Majesty of his Style, he try'd immediately to imitate it in *English*' (J. E. Spingarn, ed., *Critical Essays of the Seventeenth Century*, Oxford, 1908–9, ii. 131). This was presumably during the years when Cowley was based on Paris in the service of Queen Henrietta Maria, the wife, and after 1649 the widow, of Charles I. His collection of *Pindarique Odes* came out in 1656.

He did not adopt a regular metrical form for these. His lines vary unpredictably in length, his rhymes conform to no set pattern, and his stanzas differ considerably from one another in size. Since his lines are metrical, and since they rhyme, he cannot be considered a writer of free verse like Walt Whitman, Ezra Pound, or D. H. Lawrence. Nevertheless, his irregular metrical verse has seemed to some critics to allow those who use it too much licence. Dr Johnson deplored its widespread influence: 'This lax and lawless versification so much concealed the deficiencies of the barren, and flattered the laziness of the idle, that it immediately overspread our books of poetry; all the boys and girls caught the pleasing fashion, and they that could do nothing else could write like Pindar' (*Lives of the Poets*, 'Abraham Cowley').

Cowley did not originate this freely rhymed and freely metrical verse. Many of his English predecessors had written in it; George Herbert, for example, had handled it with great sensitivity and flexibility to record an intimate personal conflict in 'The Collar'. But Cowley certainly popularized it as the vehicle for rendering what he and others believed to be Pindar's style and manner.

We need not assume, as did many critics in the past, that Cowley discerned no regularity whatsoever in Pindar's poetic forms. His remarks in the 'Preface' to his *Pindarique Odes* concerning his versions of 'Nemean I' and 'Olympian II' make it clear that, for better or worse, he showed his discipleship by seeking to follow the spirit rather than the letter of his original:

> If a man should undertake to translate *Pindar* word for word, it would be thought that one *Mad man* had translated *another*; as may appear, when he that understands not the *Original*, reads the verbal Traduction of him into *Latin Prose*, than which nothing seems more *Raving*. And sure, *Rhyme*, without the addition of *Wit*, and the *Spirit* of *Poetry* . . . would but make it ten times more *Distracted* than it is in *Prose*. We must consider in *Pindar* the great difference of time betwixt his age and ours, which changes, as in *Pictures*, at least the *Colours* of *Poetry*, the no less difference betwixt the *Religions* and *Customs* of our Countrys, and a thousand particularities of places,

persons, and manners, which do but confusedly appear to our Eyes at so great a distance. And lastly, (which were enough alone for my purpose) we must consider that our Ears are strangers to the Musick of his *Numbers*, which sometimes (especially in *Songs* and *Odes*) almost without any thing else, makes an excellent *Poet*; for though the *Grammarians* and *Criticks* have laboured to reduce his Verses into regular feet and measures (as they have also those of the *Greek* and *Latine Comedies*) yet in effect they are little better than *Prose* to our Ears. And I would gladly know what applause our best pieces of *English Poesie* could expect from a *Frenchman* or *Italian*, if converted faithfully, and word for word, into *French* or *Italian Prose*.

Cowley's understanding of Pindar's metre was certainly limited· Indeed, no one in modern times understood it correctly until the nineteenth century. But his refraining from imitating the triadic form was undoubtedly deliberate. He chose to employ a kind of verse that would leave him as free as possible to recreate, both in his two translations and in his numerous original odes, what he took to be the essential qualities of Pindar's poetry: its wild and impulsive character, its frequent, abrupt digressions, its daring images, and its sometimes harsh utterance. But Cowley certainly failed to appreciate Pindar's craftsmanship and control; and, in seeking to accommodate to the taste of his own age what he supposed to be the main Pindaric qualities, he produced poetry that is intelligently conceived, fluent and ingenious, that declaims a little too determinedly, and that sometimes swells with bombast. It is the poetry of a baroque artist of genuine but mediocre talent.

The fourth and last stanza of 'The Resurrection' simultaneously describes the bold poetry Cowley was trying to write and exemplifies the frigid verse which was often the best he could manage:

> Stop, stop, my *Muse*, allay thy vig'orous heat,
> Kindled at a *Hint* so Great.
> Hold thy *Pindarique Pegasus* closely in,
> Which does to *rage* begin,
> And this steep *Hill* would gallop up with violent course,

> 'Tis an unruly, and a *hard-Mouth'd Horse*,
>> Fierce, and unbroken yet,
>> Impatient of the *Spur* or *Bit*.
> Now *praunces* stately, and anon *flies* o're the place,
> Disdains the *servile Law* of any settled *pace*,
> *Conscious* and *proud* of his own *natural force*.
>> 'Twill no *unskilful Touch* endure,
> But flings *Writer* and *Reader* too that *sits* not *sure*.

The lines composing this stanza vary in length from three to six metrical feet. Neither they nor the rhymes form any strictly regular pattern, though there is a tendency for the rhymes to occur in couplets. In metrical and rhyming pattern, as well as in total length, the other three stanzas differ from this and from one another. But these liberties do not enable Cowley to achieve the '*way* and *manner* of speaking' that he ascribed to Pindar. Rhetoric deputizes for passion, and fancy for imagination.

In the second stanza of 'The Muse', he describes how the goddess takes her flight

> Where never *Foot* of *Man*, or *Hoof* of *Beast*,
>> The passage prest,
>> Where never *Fish* did *fly*,
> And with short silver *wings* cut the low liquid *Sky*.
>> Where *Bird* with painted *Oars* did nere
> *Row* through the trackless *Ocean* of the *Air*. . . .

The self-delighting playfulness of this would be appropriate enough in a popular song, but it is far removed from the true Pindaric dignity:

> Joy is the best healer
> Of labours decided, and Songs,
> The Muses' wise daughters,
> Charm her forth by their touch,
> Nor does warm water so drench and soften the limbs
> As praise joined to the harp.

> Longer than actions lives the word,
> Whatsoever, with the Graces' help,
> The tongue picks out from the depths of the mind.
>
> ('Nemean IV': trans. Bowra)

In 1685 John Dryden (1631–1700) noted the spread of the irregular Pindaric ode. He ascribed this to its 'seeming easiness' but held that hardly anyone apart from Cowley had yet handled it with success. Cowley had 'the warmth and vigour of fancy, the masterly figures, and the copiousness of imagination' which the form requires. But even he fell short in certain respects; 'somewhat of the purity of English, somewhat of more equal thoughts, somewhat of sweetness in the numbers [i.e., the metre], in one word, somewhat of a finer turn and more lyrical verse, is yet wanting.'

> Since Pindar was the prince of lyric poets, let me have leave to say that, in imitating him, our numbers should, for the most part, be lyrical: for variety, or rather where the majesty of thought requires it, they may be stretched to the English heroic of five feet, and to the French Alexandrine of six. But the ear must preside and direct the judgment to the choice of numbers: without the nicety of this, the harmony of Pindaric verse can never be complete; the cadency of one line must be a rule to that of the next; and the sound of the former must slide gently into that which follows, without leaping from one extreme into another. It must be done like the shadowings of a picture, which fall by degrees into a darker colour.
>
> ('Preface' to *Sylvae*)

Dryden demonstrates his own feeling for this harmony in 'Threnodia Augustalis' (1685), a poem occasioned by the death of Charles II. Though this was his first Pindaric ode, he had been publishing poetry for more than a quarter of a century and was a highly experienced craftsman. The last of his eighteen irregular stanzas ends not with an ample line of six or seven metrical feet, such as Cowley had favoured, but with a brief, emphatic line of three feet. Yet this short line can easily be heard as extending the four-foot line that precedes it into a seven-foot line which completes the sequence established in the lines of four, five, and six feet which lead up to it. So we have a hint of an ample, resounding conclusion simultaneously with an actual presentation that is compact and epigrammatic. The lines speak of the restoration of English sea-power:

> While starting from his Oozy Bed,
> Th' asserted Ocean rears his reverend Head;
> To View and Recognize his ancient Lord again:
> And with a willing hand, restores
> The *Fasces* of the Main.

The ease and assurance of this ending are characteristic of the mature Dryden.

But Dryden's finest irregular Pindarics are 'To the Pious Memory Of the Accomplisht Young Lady Mrs Anne Killigrew' (1686), 'A Song for St Cecilia's Day, 1687', and 'Alexander's Feast; or The Power of Musique' (1697). The second and third of these were written for two of the annual celebrations of St Cecilia's Day. The saint had a special association with church music, and in particular with the organ, which she was sometimes said to have invented, so the programme on each occasion from 1683 onwards took the form of a church service followed by an entertainment in which an ode, written and composed for the occasion, had an important place. In style, these odes reflect the growing taste of their time for Italian music, which was dignified, emotional, and decorative.

In the central stanzas of the ode of 1687, Dryden puts on a display of virtuosity. His theme is the power of music to 'raise and quell' every human emotion. He starts with the trumpet and drum, suggesting their effect by an impetuous anapaestic metre, by a diction which amplifies the onomatopoeia, and by a series of vigorously martial images. For the flute and lute, he reverts to iambic metre; the lines move gently and unassertively, assonance contributing to the onomatopoeia, until the stanza dies away in the *rallentando* of its long last line. Violins suggest to Dryden almost insanely violent personal passions. After a single iambic line introducing the instruments, he hastens the tempo and switches without a jolt into a plunging trochaic metre, with alliteration pointing important stresses and with onomatopoeia again contributing, this time to evoke the insistency of the music. The whole passage is a copybook illustration of what Dryden meant when he said that in irregular Pindarics 'the ear must preside and direct the judgement to the choice of numbers':

> The TRUMPETS loud Clangor
>   Excites us to Arms
> With shrill Notes of Anger
>   And mortal Alarms.
> The double double double beat
>   Of the thundring DRUM
>   Cryes, heark the Foes come;
> Charge, Charge, 'tis too late to retreat.
>
>   The soft complaining FLUTE
>   In dying Notes discovers
>   The Woes of hopeless Lovers,
> Whose Dirge is whisper'd by the warbling LUTE.
>
> Sharp VIOLINS proclaim
> Their jealous Pangs, and Desperation,
> Fury, frantick Indignation,
> Depth of Pains, and height of Passion,
>   For the fair, disdainful Dame.

But 'Alexander's Feast' is Dryden's crowning achievement in this kind. It describes how Timotheus by his music sways the emotions of Alexander the Great at a feast celebrating the conquest of Persia. In turns, Alexander supposes himself divine, revels in drinking, pities his fallen enemy Darius, feels love for his mistress Thais, and lusts for revenge against his Persian foes. Though Dryden's lines vary more widely than ever both in length and in metre, his ear and judgement were never more sures. Repetitions of words and phrases, which in isolation could easily seem extravagant, entirely justify themselves in their contexts. The writing is versatile, elegant, serene; at the same time it is virile, bold, even flamboyant.

The fourth stanza starts as Timotheus concludes his 'Praise of *Bacchus*':

> Sooth'd with the Sound the King grew vain;
>> Fought all his Battails o'er again;
> And thrice He routed all his Foes; and thrice He slew the slain.
>> The Master saw the Madness rise;
>> His glowing Cheeks, his ardent Eyes;
>> And while He Heav'n and Earth defy'd
>> Chang'd his hand, and check'd his Pride.
>>> He chose a Mournful Muse
>>> Soft Pity to infuse:
>> He sung *Darius* Great and Good,
>>> By too severe a Fate,
>> Fallen, fallen, fallen, fallen,
>>> Fallen from his high Estate
>>> And weltring in his Blood:
>> Deserted at his utmost Need,
>> By those his former Bounty fed:
>> On the bare Earth expos'd He lyes,
>> With not a Friend to close his Eyes.
>
> With down-cast Looks the joyless Victor sate,
>> Revolveing in his alter'd Soul
>>> The various Turns of Chance below;
>> And, now and then, a Sigh he stole;
>>> And Tears began to flow.

Here again we find Dryden manipulating his metres with conspicuous skill. As elsewhere, alliteration reinforces many of his stresses; the example in the seventh line contributes, along with the simultaneous brief imposition of a trochaic rhythm, to the sharp deceleration and momentary halt which precede the musician's choice of a 'Mournful Muse'. Dryden must have meant the king's flushed review of his past victories to be just a little laughable; 'thrice He slew the slain' forbids us to take it otherwise. In the poem as a whole the extremes through which Alexander passes not only testify to the power of music but also imply a comment upon the conqueror's whole career.

Dryden thought 'Alexander's Feast' his best poem, and many readers have called it the greatest ode in the language. Romantic readers, on the other hand, have often decried it for its lack of 'sincerity', or intimate self-revelation; Elizabeth Barrett Browning, for instance, considered it commonplace. Even Dryden's extraordinary virtuosity has been dismissed as mere craftsmanship. But the life's work of W. H. Auden has taught us not to draw too rigid a line between craftsmanship and art; and when craftsmanship is as superb as Dryden's in 'Alexander's Feast' surely only prejudice can cause us to withhold high praise.

In 1697, 'Alexander's Feast' was sung to a setting by Jeremiah Clarke, which has perished. Some decades later, G. F. Handel composed a setting for it. This has survived and is still performed from time to time.

By writing the poems we have been reviewing, Dryden made the irregular ode an accepted and interesting form. Many took it up during the century that followed the composition of 'Alexander's Feast', believing it a suitable vehicle for dignified themes: 'religious fervor, patriotic zeal, philosophic reflection, and biographical tribute' (Shuster, p. 147). But successes were rare. Late in the century, William Cowper had to admit that 'we have few good English odes' (letter dated 4 August 1783).

Our Poets Laureate were among the more frequent users of the form. Throughout the eighteenth century and into the early part

of the nineteenth century, they turned out annual Birthday Odes
and New Year Odes for royalty. Many of these deliver their
stately compliments in the 'lax and lawless versification' of the
irregular Pindaric; they were often ridiculed at the time and can
excite little interest today. When offering the Laureateship to
Thomas Gray in 1757, the Lord Chamberlain tried to tempt him
by suggesting that the New Year and Birthday Odes might no
longer be required. But Gray refused the offer, and the new
Laureate, William Whitehead, dutifully performed the set tasks
as his predecessors had done. It was Robert Southey, appointed
in 1813, who earned the gratitude of his successors by shifting
the emphasis from writing odes 'at stated times and upon stated
subjects' to celebrating 'great public events ... as the spirit
moved' (letter dated 5 September 1813).

THE TRUE PINDARIC FORM

William Congreve (1670–1729), our most accomplished author
of comedies of manners, tried his hand at the irregular Pindaric
before reacting against the influence of Cowley and turning to the
strict triadic form. No memorable writer had employed it since
Ben Jonson, and no other was to do so until Thomas Gray (1716–
71) produced 'The Progress of Poesy' and 'The Bard'.

The first of these celebrates the power of poetry and glimpses
its operations in the savage state, in Greece, in Rome, and in
England. The second tells how a solitary Welsh bard curses the
conquering Edward I and foretells the misfortunes which await
the king's descendants. He predicts finally the glorious reign of
Elizabeth I, whose 'eye proclaims her of the Briton-Line'.

The broad sweep and the patriotic and other important implica-
tions of these subjects evidently invited Pindaric treatment; and
Gray did not stop at the adoption of the triadic structure. The
last epode of 'The Bard' opens with a vision of the literary glories
of the Elizabethan age and its successor:

c

> The verse adorn again
> Fierce War, and faithful Love,
> And Truth severe, by fairy Fiction drest.
> In buskin'd measures move
> Pale Grief, and pleasing Pain,
> With Horrour, Tyrant of the throbbing breast.
> A Voice, as of the Cherub-Choir,
> Gales from blooming Eden bear;
> And distant warblings lessen on my ear,
> That lost in long futurity expire.

The second of these lines echoes a phrase from the first stanza of the introduction to *The Faerie Queene*, and the words 'fairy Fiction' confirm that Gray intends an allusion to Edmund Spenser. In this context, the mention of 'buskin'd [i.e., tragic] measures' and of the feelings which they express inevitably brings Shakespeare to mind. The last four lines similarly suggest Milton, and the 'Gales from blooming Eden' are evidently the 'gentle gales' which blow from Eden in *Paradise Lost*, iv. 153–65. None of the three poets is actually named. Gray, like Pindar, prefers oblique allusions, which give an aloof dignity to his lines. The inversion of three successive clauses in the passage quoted contributes to this same effect, as does the elaborateness of the diction.

The oblique allusions and swift transitions of 'The Bard' have baffled many readers, as have the similar attributes of Pindar's odes. But from the start Gray's regular Pindarics have evoked admiration, even if sometimes reluctant, for their rich diction, their striking imagery, and their consistently lofty tone. The bard's vision of his massacred fellows displays the characteristic qualities:

> Cold is Cadwallo's tongue,
> That hush'd the stormy main:
> Brave Urien sleeps upon his craggy bed:
> Mountains, ye mourn in vain
> Modred, whose magic song
> Made huge Plinlimmon bow his cloud-top'd head.

On dreary Arvon's shore they lie,
Smear'd with gore, and ghastly pale:
Far, far aloof th' affrighted ravens sail;
The famish'd Eagle screams, and passes by.
Dear lost companions of my tuneful art,
Dear, as the light that visits these sad eyes,
Dear, as the ruddy drops that warm my heart,
Ye died amidst your dying country's cries –
No more I weep. They do not sleep.
On yonder cliffs, a griesly band,
I see them sit, they linger yet,
Avengers of their native land:
With me in dreadful harmony they join,
And weave with bloody hands the tissue of thy line.

According to Dr Johnson, however, we have here only 'the puerilities of obsolete mythology'. He protests that when we learn of the deeds attributed to Cadwallo and Modred 'attention recoils from the repetition of a tale that, even when it was first heard, was heard with scorn'. In his view, 'the two Sister Odes' are disfigured 'by glittering accumulations of ungraceful ornaments; they strike, rather than please; the images are magnified by affectation; the language is laboured into harshness. The mind of the writer seems to work with unnatural violence.' Johnson finds 'a kind of cumbrous splendor' in Gray's odes generally (*Lives of the Poets*, 'Thomas Gray').

These include an irregular 'Ode for Music', an elegant mock-ode 'On the Death of a Favourite Cat Drowned in a Tub of Gold Fishes', and an 'Ode on a Distant Prospect of Eton College' that recalls the half-dozen monostrophic odes of Pindar himself. But after Gray little life remained in the strictly Pindaric tradition in England. During subsequent centuries the irregular ode was to attract several distinguished practitioners. These would use it in their own fashions, however, and not in emulation of the Greek lyrist.

3
Horatian Odes

Unlike Pindar, Horace was known throughout the Middle Ages
But imitation of him became common only in the sixteenth
century. Henry Howard, Earl of Surrey (1517–47), produced one
of the earliest English versions of an Horatian ode. Despite much
clumsiness, his rendering of the tenth ode of Book II has something
of the density and compactness of the original. Its celebration of
the 'mean estate' may have helped to establish the theme in the
subsequent poetry of the period.

Drayton's odes testify to Horace's influence; and the success
of Jonson's poem on Sir Henry Morison should not stop us
from seeing that in general the cool equanimity of Horace was
closer to his poetic temperament than was the burning
passion of Pindar. When he exhorts himself to persist in
writing well, despite the popular preference for shoddy work
he does so with a reserve that makes his 'pitious scorne' utterly
withering:

> What though the greedie Frie [i.e., rabble]
>   Be taken with false Baytes
> Of worded Balladrie,
>   And thinke it Poësie?
>   They die with their conceits,
> And only pitious scorne, upon their folly waites.
>
> ('An Ode. To himselfe')

Jonson's example influenced some of the younger men. 'An
Ode to Mr Anthony Stafford to hasten him into the Country'
by Thomas Randolph (1605–35), is a clear instance; and a more
famous 'son of Ben', Robert Herrick (1591–1674), has left us

not only five odes so named by himself but also other poems that might well have been so named. Like Randolph, he follows Jonson in favouring complex and elaborate stanza-forms for them. In secular odes, his characteristic manner is cheerful, familiar, and genial; in short, thoroughly Horatian:

> Here we securely live, and eate
>   The Creame of meat;
>   And keep eternal fires,
> By which we sit, and doe Divine
>   As Wine
>   And Rage inspires. . . .
>
> Then cause we *Horace* to be read,
>   Which sung, or seyd,
>   A Goblet, to the brim,
> Of Lyrick Wine, both swell'd and crown'd,
>   A Round
>   We quaffe to him.
>
> Thus, thus, we live, and spend the houres
>   In Wine and Flowers:
>   And make the frollick yeere,
> The Month, the Week, the instant Day
>   To stay
>   The longer here.
>
>   ('An Ode to Sir Clipsebie Crew)'

Milton, who admired Jonson but was no 'son of Ben', translated Horace's poem addressed to Pyrrha. He also wrote sonnets which are very like Horatian odes: '*Lawrence* of vertuous Father vertuous Son', for example, and '*Cyriack*, whose Grandsire on the Royal Bench', and 'Captain or Colonel, or Knight in Arms'.

But in one of the greatest poems of the seventeenth century Andrew Marvell (1621–78) chose to emulate Horace's longer and graver odes in praise of Augustus. 'An Horatian Ode upon

Cromwel's Return from Ireland' is the work of a singularly detached and open-minded supporter of the Parliamentarian régime.

During the sixteen-forties, the English Civil War had ended in a victory for the Parliament, which Cromwell served. King Charles I had been beheaded in 1649. Cromwell's ruthless subjugation of Ireland occupied him from August 1649 to May 1650. In July 1650, only two months after his return to England, he was to cross the northern border on a preventive campaign against Scotland. He was to suppress an attempted restoration of the monarchy in 1651 and to become Lord Protector in 1653.

Evidently writing in the early summer of 1650, Marvell celebrates this man's virtues. He sees him as having agreed to leave his simple and apparently contented life in rustic obscurity in order to undertake important military and political duties. Cromwell's disciplined obedience in discharging these, in conjunction with his other active and contemplative virtues, proves him fit to exercise the highest authority. Even the Irish, says Marvell implausibly, admit 'How good he is, how just'. But his courage, justice, and devotion to public duty do not complete the account. Marvell hints that Cromwell could also be something of a Machiavellian. He does so by a veiled allusion to a report which modern historians think unfounded but which was current at the time: that Cromwell had connived at Charles's escape from Hampton Court to Carisbrooke Castle a year or so before his execution, knowing well that if the King took the opportunity he would be landing himself in a more precarious situation.

Even thus qualified, Marvell's praise of Cromwell's virtues is not the whole truth he has to tell about him. He also sees him very much as Byron and many of his contemporaries saw Napoleon, that is, as the embodiment of an awe-inspiring and irresistible natural force. He compares this with the lightning that breaks its way out of an enclosing cloud and blasts the head of Caesar himself. There would be no sense in resisting or blaming – or, presumably, praising – such a manifestation:

> 'Tis Madness to resist or blame
> The force of angry Heavens flame.

By such force, Cromwell has 'cast the Kingdome old/Into another Mold'. Perhaps he infringed 'antient Rights' in doing so. But such rights 'hold or break/As Men are strong or weak'. Marvell accepts the necessity of the revolution that has occurred and acknowledges that force has brought it about. Force, he concludes, must now defend what it has achieved:

> The same *Arts* that did *gain*
> A *Pow'r* must it *maintain*.

The most eminent victim of this man and this force, Charles himself, receives a moving tribute from the poet. Cromwell, he says, ensnared Charles at Carisbrooke Castle,

> That thence the *Royal Actor* born
> The *Tragick Scaffold* might adorn:
>   While round the armed Bands
>   Did clap their bloody hands.
> *He* nothing common did or mean
> Upon that memorable Scene:
>   But with his keener Eye
>   The Axes edge did try:
> Nor call'd the *Gods* with vulgar spight
> To vindicate his helpless Right,
>   But bow'd his comely Head,
>   Down as upon a Bed.

The courage and dignity with which the '*Royal Actor*' plays his tragic part tend to modify our approval of Cromwell and our acquiescence in the triumph of force.

Despite its brevity, the 'Horatian Ode' has an extraordinary comprehensiveness. It records insights into an historical crisis and the persons involved which are not easily reconcilable with one another. Though its author's temperate endorsement of current developments is clear, he refuses to stifle such perceptions as may make against it. He has no wish to be a polemicist. He is open-minded and flexible. As a politician, he is sincerely committed to the support of the Parliamentarian régime, but as an artist he is detached, poised, judicious. As we read, we find it natural to recall Horace's fine Actium ode (I. xxxvii).

Contemporary Royalists testified involuntarily to Marvell's freedom from partisan passion. During the evil days of the sixteen-fifties they circulated the poem surreptitiously among themselves; but twenty-one years after the restoration of the monarchy they found its Parliamentarianism too bold for its publication to be permissible.

Cowley was another Horatian. But his taste for a simple, studious, and quietly sociable life, safely removed from the hazards of the busy world, seems to have drawn him to the more personal and familiar of the odes. These were evidently in his mind when he formulated his ideal in stanzas which are more diffuse than anything Horace would have written but probably truer to Cowley's own nature than his irregular Pindarics were to be:

> This only grant me, that my means may lye
> Too low for Envy, for Contempt too high.
>> Some Honor I would have
> Not from great deeds, but good alone.
> The unknown are better than ill known.
>> Rumour can ope' the Grave,
> Acquaintance I would have, but when 't depends
> Not on the number, but the choice of Friends.
>
> Books should, not business entertain the Light,
> And sleep, as undisturb'd as Death, the Night.
>> My House a Cottage, more

Then Palace, and should fitting be
For all my Use, no Luxury.
  My Garden painted o're
With Natures hand, not Arts; and pleasures yeild,
Horace might envy in his Sabine field.

('A Vote')

Cowley here employs a fairly elaborate stanza-form as the vehicle for thoughts and sentiments of a broadly Horatian kind. His predecessors, Jonson, Randolph, and Herrick, did much the same. But Horace composed most of his odes in simple and precise four-line stanzas. Milton reproduced one of these forms pretty closely in his version of the Pyrrha ode, and Marvell wrote his 'Horatian Ode' in what he evidently intended as an English equivalent of the particular Latin four-line pattern he had in mind. In 'An Ode, upon occasion of His Majesties Proclamation in the Year 1630. Commanding the Gentry to reside upon their Estates in the Countrey', the very title of which advertises its Horatian theme, Sir Richard Fanshawe (1608–66) used the four-line stanza in which Alexander Pope (1688–1714) was to write one of his few lyrical poems. Pope's 'Ode on Solitude' is short enough to be quoted in full:

> Happy the man, whose wish and care
> A few paternal acres bound,
> Content to breathe his native air,
>   In his own ground.
>
> Whose herds with milk, whose fields with bread,
> Whose flocks supply him with attire,
> Whose trees in summer yield him shade,
>   In winter fire.
>
> Blest! who can unconcern'dly find
> Hours, days, and years slide soft away,
> In health of body, peace of mind,
>   Quiet by day,

> Sound sleep by night; study and ease
> Together mix'd; sweet recreation,
> And innocence, which most does please,
>   With meditation.
>
> Thus let me live, unseen, unknown;
> Thus unlamented let me dye;
> Steal from the world, and not a stone
>   Tell where I lye.

The Horatianism of this seems to have come to Pope largely through Cowley. Pope expresses it with conviction in stanzas which are variously and exquisitely cadenced. He claimed to have written the poem when he was 'about twelve years old'. Even if he revised it later, as seems likely, it remains a remarkable achievement.

Eighteenth-century Horatian odes tend to be composed in fairly brief and simple stanzas. In one of the best-known, Matthew Prior (1664–1721) employs the iambic tetrameter quatrain. This 'Ode', too, is short enough to be quoted in full:

> The Merchant, to secure his Treasure,
>   Conveys it in a borrow'd Name:
> EUPHELIA serves to grace my Measure;
>   But CLOE is my real Flame.
>
> My softest Verse, my darling Lyre
>   Upon EUPHELIA's Toilet lay;
> When CLOE noted her Desire,
>   That I should sing, that I should play.
>
> My Lyre I tune, my Voice I raise;
>   But with my Numbers mix my Sighs:
> And whilst I sing EUPHELIA's Praise,
>   I fix my Soul on CLOE's Eyes.
>
> Fair CLOE blush'd: EUPHELIA frown'd:
>   I sung and gaz'd: I play'd and trembl'd:
> And VENUS to the LOVES around
>   Remark'd, how ill We all dissembl'd.

The Horace who is in question here is not a seeker after rural retirement but a sophisticated observer of, and participant in, the human comedy. Prior's simple language and easy manner should not lead us to underrate his skill. Gradually abbreviating his syntactical units, he introduces his verbs more and more frequently as the poem proceeds, and largely by this means he achieves his telling climax half-way through the last stanza. Just as his starting with a feminine rhyme has signalled that he is not wholly in earnest, so his closing with another feminine rhyme helps to confirm the tone of polite mockery which the poem exists to express.

Both as a lover of retirement on his Sabine farm and as a genial observer of the human comedy, Horace deeply affected our eighteenth-century poets. His influence occasionally took unexpected forms. Isaac Watts (1674–1748), for example, some years before publishing his well-known *Divine Songs for the Use of Children*, employed the Horatian Sapphic stanza for a lurid vision of the Day of Judgement:

> Hopeless Immortals! how they scream and shiver
> While Devils push them to the Pit wide yawning
> Hideous and gloomy, to receive them headlong
>   Down to the Centre.
>   ('The Day of Judgment. An Ode')

Watts has transformed the urbane Roman Epicurean into a hellfire preacher.

With Horace's Alcaic stanza in mind, William Collins (1721–59) borrowed for his 'Ode to Evening' the unrhymed form used in the Miltonic Pyrrha ode. Collins creates his personification of Evening mainly by an exact and highly evocative pictorial presentation of her concomitants. Proving himself to possess the 'incomparable and infallible eye for landscape' that Swinburne praised, he asks the 'calm Vot'ress' to lead him

> where some sheety lake
> Cheers the lone heath, or some time-hallow'd pile,
>   Or up-land fallows grey
>   Reflects it's last cool gleam.
> But when chill blust'ring winds, or driving rain,
> Forbid my willing feet, be mine the hut,
>   That from the mountain's side,
>   Views wilds, and swelling floods,
> And hamlets brown, and dim-discover'd spires,
> And hears their simple bell, and marks o'er all
>   Thy dewy fingers draw
>   The gradual dusky veil.

While deeply indebted to Classical models, Collins exhibits
in such passages as this a sensibility that points forward to Rom-
anticism. With the emergence of this new outlook, it becomes less
easy and less useful to trace the development of the ode in terms
of the Pindaric and Horatian styles. Odes which apparently owe
someting to both traditions, or very little to either, become more
common. Before we move on to these newer modes, however, a
couple of deliberate reversions to the Horatian manner by nine-
teenth-century poets claim our attention.

Matthew Arnold (1822–88) wrote an 'Horatian Echo' in 1847.
With urbane detachment, he dismisses the political concerns which
were exciting his fellows as Europe moved towards 'the year of
revolutions':

> Omit, omit, my simple friend,
> Still to enquire how parties tend,
> Or what we fix with foreign powers.
> If France and we are really friends,
> And what the Russian Czar intends,
>   Is no concern of ours.

Though he drops a little below this level in what follows, the
gentle melancholy with which he voices the *carpe diem* theme
sustains the Horatian note to the end.

Alfred Tennyson (1809–92) addressed 'The Daisy' to his wife: 'In a metre which I invented, representing in some measure the grandest of metres, the Horatian Alcaic.' He modified the stanza slightly for three other epistolary poems. Of these, 'To the Rev. F. D. Maurice' invites his friend, the godfather of his son, to visit him in the Isle of Wight. Maurice, who was a theologian of great distinction, had just been forced by a council of King's College, London, to resign his professorship because he denied the doctrine of eternal punishment. Tennyson, too, found that doctrine abhorrent.

His invitation is cordial. It has an Horatian ease and elegance and a Tennysonian affectionateness and charm. The poem is both an echo and an original creation:

> Come, when no graver cares employ,
> Godfather, come and see your boy:
>   Your presence will be sun in winter,
> Making the little one leap for joy.
>
> For, being of that honest few,
> Who give the Fiend himself his due,
>   Should eighty-thousand college-councils
> Thunder 'Anathema', friend, at you;
>
> Should all our churchmen foam in spite
> At you, so careful of the right,
>   Yet one lay-hearth would give you welcome
> (Take it and come) to the Isle of Wight;
>
> Where, far from noise and smoke of town,
> I watch the twilight falling brown
>   All round a careless-ordered garden
> Close to the ridge of a noble down.
>
> You'll have no scandal while you dine,
> But honest talk and wholesome wine,
>   And only hear the magpie gossip
> Garrulous under a roof of pine:

> For groves of pine on either hand,
> To break the blast of winter, stand;
> 　And further on, the hoary Channel
> Tumbles a billow on chalk and sand.

In what follows, Tennyson touches on the hostilities between Russia and Turkey that were soon to culminate in the Crimean War and on his friend's Christian concern with social problems. He achieves a tone that, while urbane, is earnest; and he communicates his warm regard for Maurice and his ready participation in Maurice's interests with a calm geniality that has no equivalent in Arnold's rather academic exercise.

4
Nineteenth-Century Odes

The examples we have considered so far allow us to think of an ode as a poem of a grave and noble kind on a theme of acknowledged importance; it is likely to be of fair length, and either cast in the form of an address or evoked by some particular occasion. Naturally, individual specimens may deviate appreciably from this general account, and a poem as light and as brief as that in which Prior describes his involvement with the rival ladies may receive the title. Though we should find certain poems difficult to classify, we can make a general distinction between an ode and a song. Etymology gives no help here, since 'ode' is itself a Greek word meaning 'song' that has come to us through the Latin 'oda'. But our actual usage shows that we think of a song as comparatively simple and spontaneous and of an ode as comparatively elaborate and formal. These attributes of the ode need not imply any lack of emotion. On the contrary, many odes are characterized by serious reflection upon feelings of very great strength.

It is with some such general account in mind that we must approach the odes of a period in which the Pindaric and Horatian traditions become much less clear and distinct. No doubt odes in both traditional styles were still appearing. But they rarely came from poets of the rank that alone concerns us here. Such poets might write irregular odes and they might write formal odes. But they were unlikely to be thinking of Pindar or Horace in connection with them.

Admittedly, things were different on the Continent. Goethe and Schiller in Germany and Victor Hugo in France produced odes in the Pindaric tradition, and Hölderlin was the most ardent Pindarist of all. But in England the irregular ode and the formal ode had by this time achieved effective independence of the Classical authors to whom they owed their conception. Milton had known Pindar well; his Latin Pindaric, 'Ad Joannem Rousium Oxoniensis Academiae Bibliothecarium' (1646), shows as much. William Wordsworth, too, had a copy of Pindar in his library. But when this was offered for sale the author of the best-known irregular ode of the Romantic period in England was found never to have read it.

THE ROMANTICS

William Wordsworth (1770–1850) wrote the first four stanzas of this poem in 1802, resumed work on it after an interval of more than two years during which there occurred the death of his brother John, and published it under the simple title 'Ode' in 1807. The sub-title, 'Intimations of Immortality from Recollections of Early Childhood', was added much later.

In the poem he records an emotional crisis in his own life; he reflects upon the process of growing to maturity as known to all of us; and he finds grounds in his experience for affirming a belief in immortality. The first four stanzas define his personal problem. Whereas a 'celestial light' seemed once to apparel all that he beheld, 'The things which I have seen I now can see no more'.

> The Rainbow comes and goes,
> And lovely is the Rose,
> The Moon doth with delight
> Look round her when the heavens are bare,
> Waters on a starry night
> Are beautiful and fair;
> The sunshine is a glorious birth;
> But yet I know, where'er I go,
> That there hath past away a glory from the earth.

He observes how nature rejoices at the return of spring, and he responds to her rejoicing. But repetitions, 'I feel – I feel it all' and 'I hear, I hear, with joy I hear', make the response seem willed, the ecstasy deliberate, and we are not surprised when he ends this first part with the questions,

> Whither is fled the visionary gleam?
> Where is it now, the glory and the dream?

He opens the second by taking up two Platonic notions: that the immortality of the soul implies a prenatal existence, and that some recollection of this earlier state survives the trauma of birth. If these are true, it follows that 'Heaven lies about us in our infancy'. But the 'celestial light' is ours only for a time.

> Shades of the prison-house begin to close
>   Upon the growing Boy,
> But He beholds the light, and whence it flows,
>   He sees it in his joy;
> The Youth, who daily farther from the east
>   Must travel, still is Nature's Priest,
>   And by the vision splendid
>   Is on his way attended;
> At length the Man perceives it die away,
> And fade into the light of common day.

The 'glory and the dream' have succumbed to earthly interests. As young children, however, we still enjoyed the visionary outlook and the thoughtless conviction of immortality which relates so closely to it. Wordsworth devotes stanzas v to viii to the calm but impassioned exposition of these metaphysical ideas. They enable him to infer, from the 'visionary gleam' which things once had for him, the belief in immortality that his recent bereavement has made urgent.

But has not life been unbearably impoverished by the loss of the 'visionary gleam'? The third part of the poem, consisting of

D

the last three stanzas, explains why this is not so. Though the gleam 'is fled', Wordsworth gives thanks that he yet remembers his 'fugitive' early experience,

> those obstinate questionings
> Of sense and outward things,
> Fallings from us, vanishings;
> Blank misgivings of a Creature
> Moving about in worlds not realised.

The thought of such experience can renew in us our sense of the pure spirituality which was once ours:

> Hence in a season of calm weather
> Though inland far we be,
> Our Souls have sight of that immortal sea
> Which brought us hither,
> Can in a moment travel thither,
> And see the Children sport upon the shore,
> And hear the mighty waters rolling evermore.

The poet can now rejoice, having constructed something upon which to rejoice. Admittedly, he cannot recapture the hour of 'splendour in the grass, of glory in the flower'; but he has determined to find strength in what remains:

> In the primal sympathy
> Which having been must ever be;
> In the soothing thoughts that spring
> Out of human suffering;
> In the faith that looks through death,
> In years that bring the philosophic mind.

A contemplative faith has replaced the lost intuitive joy. The poet can now continue under the 'more habitual sway' of the 'Fountains, Meadows, Hills, and Groves' he has loved. He concludes:

> To me the meanest flower that blows can give
> Thoughts that do often lie too deep for tears.

There is an inwardness and earnestness about this poem, and in places an unguarded, poignant simplicity of utterance, that differentiate it sharply from the irregular Pindarics of Cowley and Dryden and the regular Pindarics of Gray. It makes even the finest of these look like *bravura* pieces, splendid, no doubt, but just a little showy. Yet it emerges from the tradition that they represent. That tradition has now grown largely independent of Classical authority, however; it has developed its own momentum as the tradition of the irregular metrical ode in English.

Another representative of it began as the verse letter to Sara Hutchinson that Samuel Taylor Coleridge (1772–1834) seems to have written immediately on becoming acquainted in 1802 with the first four stanzas – all that then existed – of Wordsworth's 'Ode'. After revision and abbreviation, this letter became 'Dejection: An Ode' (1817). The two odes resemble each other in certain ways. Both are irregular, and both are concerned with the loss of special kinds of joy. But they differ from each other, too. Wordsworth speaks of something that he believes all men must lose as they mature, and he discovers a compensation for the loss; Coleridge speaks of something that he personally is losing, his 'shaping spirit of Imagination', and for this loss there can be no compensation.

'Dejection: An Ode' is a singularly painful poem. 'A grief without a pang, void, dark, and drear', afflicts the poet. It impairs in him the spontaneous joy without which his perception of nature cannot be complete; for Coleridge both as a poet and as a philosopher saw perception as an essentially active, imaginative, creative process:

> O Lady! we receive but what we give,
> And in our life alone does Nature live:

Ours is her wedding garment, ours her shroud!
And would we aught behold, of higher worth,
Than that inanimate cold world allowed
To the poor loveless ever-anxious crowd,
Ah! from the soul itself must issue forth
A light, a glory, a fair luminous cloud
Enveloping the Earth —
And from the soul itself must there be sent
A sweet and potent voice, of its own birth,
Of all sweet sounds the life and element!

But the poet has lost the joy from which this light, this glory, should spring. In the sixth stanza, described by T. S. Eliot as 'one of the saddest of confessions that I have ever read', Coleridge explains that afflictions have so bowed him down and have so crippled his imagination that he can only resign himself in stillness and patience and divert his powers into abstract intellectual studies:

There was a time when, though my path was rough,
This joy within me dallied with distress,
And all misfortunes were but as the stuff
Whence Fancy made me dreams of happiness:
For hope grew round me, like the twining vine,
And fruits, and foliage, not my own, seemed mine.
But now afflictions bow me down to earth:
Nor care I that they rob me of my mirth;
But oh! each visitation
Suspends what nature gave me at my birth,
My shaping spirit of Imagination.
For not to think of what I needs must feel,
But to be still and patient, all I can;
And haply by abstruse research to steal
From my own nature all the natural man —
This was my sole resource, my only plan:
Till that which suits a part infects the whole,
And now is almost grown the habit of my soul.

The original verse letter enables us to relate these 'afflictions' in particular to Coleridge's unhappy marriage and his thwarted love for Sara Hutchinson, the anonymous 'Dear Lady' of 'Dejection'. In a long and able essay in *Bicentenary Wordsworth Studies* (ed. Jonathan Wordsworth, Ithaca and London, 1970), David Pirie argues that 'A Letter to [Asra]' is a richer and more moving work than 'Dejection', impressive though that is. In short, he thinks it one of Coleridge's best poems. From our present point of view, we may note with interest that Coleridge described his poem as an ode as soon as he began in some degree to obscure its personal allusions.

Nevertheless, it remains a very personal and deeply moving work. Its agonized seriousness finds expression in the long, brooding lines of which it is mainly composed. Few irregular odes are more nearly regular. Five-sixths of its lines are either iambic pentameters or alexandrines, nearly four-fifths of them iambic pentameters. In Wordsworth's 'Ode' the shorter lines can seem to leap with elation, and the constant variety implies the resiliency of the poet's spirit. Even when Coleridge seems to be achieving his greatest variety, as in the eight lines of his third stanza and the last eight lines of his seventh, he is in fact coming close to another regular form. At each point he constructs a Miltonic 'Nativity Ode' stanza, orthodox in rhyme and metre except for having an additional foot in the seventh line. His despairing acquiescence in his lot seems to favour a weary reliance upon familiar forms. But it does not inhibit the wonderful tenderness with which he speaks of his 'Dear Lady' in the eighth and last stanza.

These are not the only poems that Coleridge and Wordsworth designated odes. Coleridge's 'Ode to the Departing Year' is irregular; his 'France: An Ode' departs only once, and then but slightly, from an elaborate monostrophic form. Wordsworth wrote odes of both kinds, his best-known apart from 'Intimations of Immortality' being his monostrophic 'Ode to Duty'.

Of the younger poets of the time, George Gordon, Lord Byron (1788–1824), is at his best in his longer and often more discursive poems. But his 'Ode to Napoleon Buonaparte' has power, even if it is an assertively rhetorical rather than a poetic power. Byron had always felt an irrational admiration for Napoleon, but this went sour in 1814 when the French Emperor abdicated after military defeat instead of remaining defiant to the last. 'I mark this day!' wrote Byron in his journal on 9 April. 'Napoleon Buonaparte has abdicated the throne of the world. ... What! wait till they were in his capital, and then talk of his readiness to give up what is already gone!!' He wrote to the same effect in his ode:

> The Desolator desolate!
>   The Victor overthrown!
> The Arbiter of others' fate
>   A Suppliant for his own!
> Is it some yet imperial hope
> That with such change can calmly cope?
>   Or dread of death alone?
> To die a Prince – or live a slave –
> Thy choice is most ignobly brave!

Though Greek themes never ceased to engage the imaginations of Percy Bysshe Shelley (1792–1822) and John Keats (1795–1821), both men achieved a virtually complete independence of Classical traditions of form in the great odes which they composed towards the end of their lives. The 'Ode to the West Wind' is a rhapsodic address, 'conceived and chiefly written', as Shelley himself records, 'in a wood that skirts the Arno, near Florence, and on a day when that tempestuous wind, whose temperature is at once mild and animating, was collecting the vapours which pour down the autumnal rains':

Thou on whose stream, mid the steep sky's commotion,
Loose clouds like earth's decaying leaves are shed,
Shook from the tangled boughs of Heaven and Ocean,

Angels of rain and lightning: there are spread
On the blue surface of thine aëry surge,
Like the bright hair uplifted from the head

Of some fierce Maenad, even from the dim verge
Of the horizon to the zenith's height,
The locks of the approaching storm.

In a deservedly well-known critique of these lines, F. R. Leavis argues that there exists nothing more than a general impression of windy tumult to associate the 'loose clouds' with the 'decaying leaves' and that accordingly the 'stream' merely reinforces the sense of streaming, instead of providing the surface on which 'clouds', like 'leaves', might be 'shed'. The 'boughs', he goes on, were evidently brought to Shelley's mind by the 'leaves' in the preceding line, 'and we are not to ask what the tree is'. The Maenad simply suggests frenzied onset, and we run into difficulties if we try to imagine her with her hair streaming in front of her as she speeds 'before a still swifter gale' (*Revaluation*, London, 1936, pp. 204–5).

Leavis's point is that a closely attentive reading in which we press for the sense of these lines, and try fully to realize their imagery, can get us nowhere. Naturally, certain admirers of Shelley have tried to tell us what the tree is and to explain the meteorology of the passage. But the poem's wiser defenders agree with Leavis that it asks to be read with a relaxed attention, coupled with a ready responsiveness to the sound and connotation of each word and phrase. Where they disagree with him is in his profound conviction that such a mode of reading is reprehensible and that poetry which invites it is pernicious. Shelley is by no means the only author to have written in such a way as to make this the appropriate way of reading his verse. Swinburne and Dylan Thomas have done much the same.

In his evocative and ecstatic vein, Shelley prays the wind to disseminate the 'dead thoughts' of one whom life has 'chained and bowed':

> Scatter, as from an unextinguished hearth
> Ashes and sparks, my words among mankind!
> Be through my lips to unawakened earth
>
> The trumpet of a prophecy! O, Wind,
> If Winter comes, can Spring be far behind?

The stanzas 'To a Skylark' end with a similar longing to disperse his thoughts throughout the world. For much of this poem, Shelley is pouring out a sequence of highly suggestive images. Having asked what the skylark may be compared with, he supplies a whole series of answers:

> Like a Poet hidden
>   In the light of thought,
> Singing hymns unbidden,
>   Till the world is wrought
> To sympathy with hopes and fears it heeded not:
>
> Like a high-born maiden
>   In a palace-tower,
> Soothing her love-laden
>   Soul in secret hour
> With music sweet as love, which overflows her bower:
>
> Like a glow-worm golden
>   In a dell of dew,
> Scattering unbeholden
>   Its aëreal hue
> Among the flowers and grass, which screen it from the view!
>
> Like a rose embowered
>   In its own green leaves,

By warm winds deflowered,
　　Till the scent it gives
Makes faint with too much sweet those heavy-wingèd thieves . . .

But this exciting display has not pleased all of Shelley's readers. Leavis dismisses 'To a Skylark' as 'a mere tumbled out spate . . . of poeticalities' (p. 215).

Opinion divides less sharply on the odes of Keats. Indeed, the best of these seem at times to be regarded as above criticism. Like the two odes of Shelley just noticed, most of them are monostrophic. Keats favours fairly long and elaborate stanzas, with few lines that are not iambic pentameters, and with rhyme-schemes having some resemblance to those normally found in sonnets. He takes up the themes to which poets have returned again and again throughout the centuries: the youthful grasping at life and beauty in the face of inevitable death, the human craving for immortality despite the irresistible passage of time, and the poignant contrast between exuberant maturity and barren decline.

These conflicts receive moving expression in three odes written in about May 1819: 'Ode to a Nightingale', 'Ode on a Grecian Urn', and 'Ode on Melancholy'. Tom Keats, deeply loved and devotedly nursed by his brother John, had died in December 1818. To the poet, the world was indeed one where 'youth grows pale, and spectre-thin, and dies'. 'The weariness, the fever, and the fret' of life would reduce any thoughtful man to sorrow and 'leaden-eyed despairs'. The poet longs to escape from an existence in which 'men sit and hear each other groan' to the realm of ideal beauty suggested by the nightingale's song. For this song, repeated by singer after singer as century has followed century, is in a sense immortal. So acute is the contrast between its immortality and the precariousness of the human lot that the poet as he listens could contentedly 'cease upon the midnight with no pain'. The song he hears is

> Perhaps the self-same song that found a path
> Through the sad heart of Ruth, when, sick for home,
> She stood in tears amid the alien corn;
> The same that oft-times hath
> Charm'd magic casements, opening on the foam
> Of perilous seas, in faery lands forlorn.

The unexpected word 'forlorn' recalls him to the real world, however, and the poem ends with his half-regretful acceptance of the summons.

In the 'Ode on a Grecian Urn' he sustains to the end his rejection of the real world in favour of an ideal beauty. The figures on the urn are happily immune from trouble, change, and death. Everlastingly beautiful, they teach us that

> 'Beauty is truth, truth beauty,' – that is all
> Ye know on earth, and all ye need to know.

Though the 'Ode on Melancholy' makes no declaration as confident as this, it has likewise a clear direction. Melancholy sharpens a man's enjoyment of short-lived lovely things, and his awareness of their evanescence nourishes his melancholy. The contrast between the eternity of the principle of beauty and the impermanence of its manifestations causes the poet deep anguish, but it is an anguish that he appears to accept, even to embrace.

These odes vary considerably in feeling. All of them show the poet trying to resolve the conflict between truth and beauty. The resolution becomes most nearly effortless in a poem of serene acceptance that he wrote on 19 September 1819, the ode 'To Autumn'. Two days later, he described the season in a letter:

How beautiful the season is now – How fine the air. A temperate sharpness about it. Really, without joking, chaste weather – Dian skies – I never lik'd stubble-fields so much as now – Aye better than the chilly green of the Spring. Somehow a stubble-plain looks warm –

in the same way that some pictures look warm – This struck me so much in my Sunday's walk that I composed upon it.

Critics as different as Leavis and Robert Bridges agree in ranking 'To Autumn' first among Keats's odes. Its three eleven-line stanzas ostensibly do nothing more than describe the season; no philosophical reflections intrude. It opens with an evocation of the 'mellow fruitfulness' which results from the autumn's conspiring with the sun

> how to load and bless
> With fruit the vines that round the thatch-eves run;
> To bend with apples the moss'd cottage-trees,
> And fill all fruit with ripeness to the core.

These lines illustrate Keats's extraordinary ability to activate not only the visual imagination but also the kinaesthetic ('load', 'bend') and tactile ('moss'd') imaginations of his readers. Elsewhere the poem shows him appealing with equal success to other senses.

In the second stanza he personifies autumn as relaxed but poised and patient. Finally, he asks:

> Where are the songs of Spring? Ay, where are they?
> Think not of them, thou hast thy music too, –
> While barred clouds bloom the soft-dying day,
> And touch the stubble-plains with rosy hue;
> Then in a wailful choir the small gnats mourn
> Among the river sallows, borne aloft
> Or sinking as the light wind lives or dies;
> And full-grown lambs loud bleat from hilly bourn;
> Hedge-crickets sing; and now with treble soft
> The red-breast whistles from a garden-croft;
> And gathering swallows twitter in the skies.

These lines embody a very full imaginative realization of the objects they describe. Declaring that autumn has its songs to match those of spring, the poet recreates its clear and varied music for us. The richly onomatopoeic treatment of the choir of gnats has been too often noticed to call for analysis now. But the entire chorus has a freshness and an animation which exclude any consideration of autumn as the season merely of decline and decay. The 'full-grown lambs', in fact, lead our thoughts forward to the spring that is on the way. Keats rejoices not only in the autumn but in the very processes of life which continue through it. He has given substance to philosophical reflections which he has chosen not to formulate.

THE VICTORIANS

Evidently the finest odes of Wordsworth, Coleridge, Shelley, and Keats originated in intensely personal impulses. Wordsworth feels that his vision has lost the glory with which it shone when he was young; Coleridge dreads that private unhappiness has cost him his poetic imagination; Shelley longs, despite his weakness and frustration, to preach an optimistic gospel to mankind; and Keats experiences the agonizing discrepancy between his glimpses of an ideal beauty and his actual life of sickness and sorrow. But none of these odes remains merely personal. Each of them develops a complexity such as we should not expect to find, for example, in a song; each of them becomes reflective, even philosophical. Wordsworth discerns grounds for a faith in immortality and finds in his mature outlook a compensation for the loss of his juvenile vision; Coleridge formulates a doctrine of the creative activity of the mind; Shelley makes clear the redemptive nature of the gospel he would preach; and Keats achieves an acceptance of, and a satisfying perception of beauty in, the very processes of life itself.

The 'Ode to Memory' of Alfred Tennyson (1809–92), though not the equal of these Romantic odes, owes a good deal to them. Milton's 'Lycidas', too, was evidently in its author's mind. Tennyson rightly considered the 'Ode to Memory' 'one of the best of his early and peculiarly concentrated Nature-poems'. The element of reflection in it is slight, but the particular recollections of childhood are presented with delicacy and charm:

> Come from the woods that belt the gray hill-side,
> The seven elms, the poplars four
> That stand beside my father's door,
> And chiefly from the brook that loves
> To purl o'er matted cress and ribbed sand,
> Or dimple in the dark of rushy coves,
> Drawing into his narrow earthern urn,
>   In every elbow and turn,
> The filter'd tribute of the rough woodland,
>   O! hither lead thy feet!
> Pour round mine ears the livelong bleat
> Of the thick-fleeced sheep from wattled folds,
>   Upon the ridged wolds,
> When the first matin-song hath waken'd loud
> Over the dark dewy earth forlorn,
> What time the amber morn
> Forth gushes from beneath a low-hung cloud.

Over twenty years later, Tennyson composed a more powerful irregular ode. The Duke of Wellington died on 14 September 1852, and Tennyson published his 'Ode on the Death of the Duke of Wellington' on 16 November 1852, two days before the funeral. He revised it later. Tennyson, our most successful Poet Laureate, never did better in an official poem. He called it 'a fine rolling anthem', and such it must certainly have sounded to those contemporaries who heard him read it aloud, booming it out with the broad Lincolnshire vowels which he retained throughout his life:

> Bury the Great Duke
>   With an empire's lamentation,
> Let us bury the Great Duke
>   To the noise of the mourning of a mighty nation . . .

One would give much to have been able to hear him in the fifth stanza rolling out the long series of solemn rhymes on 'tolled'.

Tennyson rather indignantly denied that this was a 'laureate poem', maintaining that it was simply what he would in any case have wished to write of a great hero. But what he wanted to say was so close to what the public occasion called for that the distinction becomes blurred. Which is the more important when he speaks of the proceedings inside St Paul's Cathedral? The thought and imagery are unquestionably those of the author of *In Memoriam*:

> We revere, and while we hear
> The tides of Music's golden sea
> Setting toward eternity,
> Uplifted high in heart and hope are we,
> Until we doubt not that for one so true
> There must be other nobler work to do
> Than when he fought at Waterloo,
> And Victor he must ever be.
> For tho' the Giant Ages heave the hill
> And break the shore, and evermore
> Make and break, and work their will;
> Tho' world on world in myriad myriads roll
> Round us, each with different powers,
> And other forms of life than ours,
> What know we greater than the soul?
> On God and Godlike men we build our trust.

A younger poet who was for a time a close friend of Tennyson's, Coventry Patmore (1823–96), wrote a large number of irregular odes and published a collection entitled *The Unknown Eros*. His prophetic odes on public events are intolerably stilted and portentous. When Disraeli introduced and Parliament passed a bill that gave the vote to the working men in the towns and almost doubled the electorate, Patmore reacted with an ode, '1867', that starts repulsively enough for four lines to suffice:

NINETEENTH-CENTURY ODES 53

In the year of the great crime,
When the false English Nobles and their Jew,
By God demented, slew
The Trust they stood twice pledged to keep from wrong . . .

In his more personal odes, Patmore often does much better. But no man can ever have been less alert to irony. In 'Amelia', for example, he takes his second fiancée for a walk to the cemetery where his first wife lies buried. Naturally he is pleased when Amelia speaks affectionately of her predecessor. When she has spoken, however, he adds in all innocence the catastrophic comment, 'For dear to maidens are their rivals dead.'

It is remarkable that a man with this blind side should have learned as much as Patmore evidently did learn from the English poets of the seventeenth century. Their influence is clear in such grave, courteous, and tender lyrics as 'Departure' and 'A Farewell'. In each of these, and in others like them, a strong and supple rhythmical movement unites all parts so closely as to make piecemeal quotation inadvisable. But 'Magna est Veritas', an expression of quietism which shows Patmore at his best, is short enough to be quoted in full:

> Here, in this little Bay,
> Full of tumultuous life and great repose,
> Where, twice a day,
> The purposeless, glad ocean comes and goes,
> Under high cliffs, and far from the huge town,
> I sit me down.
> For want of me the world's course will not fail;
> When all its work is done, the lie shall rot;
> The truth is great, and shall prevail,
> When none cares whether it prevail or not.

There are regular as well as irregular Victorian odes: for instance, Tennyson's Horatian stanzas 'To the Rev. F. D. Maurice' and Arnold's 'Horatian Echo', which were discussed in Chapter 3.

Further examples in both styles could easily be cited. But, while various odes by Walter Savage Landor (1775–1864), Algernon Charles Swinburne (1837–1909), Francis Thompson (1859–1907) and others would repay attention for their own sakes, they would not exhibit any radical departures from types already reviewed.

What is of more immediate interest is the fact that as we advance into the nineteenth century poets seem to grow shyer of calling their poems odes. At the same time, many poems not so labelled are distinctly ode-like and have understandably been called odes by readers and critics. Is there anything absurd in giving that name to the 'Choric Song' that forms the major part of Tennyson's 'The Lotos-Eaters'? or to Arnold's 'Dover Beach'? or to the two irregular metrical poems which Arthur Hugh Clough (1819–61) entitled 'Easter Day'? Are not the best of Swinburne's odes to be found among the poems from which he withheld the label? And what other label could reasonably be attached to 'The Wreck of the Deutschland' of Gerard Manley Hopkins (1844–89)?

But a study of the ode which based itself upon whatever poems its author chose to call odes would give that author too tempting an opportunity of merely illustrating his own prejudices. Nearly all the poems discussed in the present volume were originally entitled odes, or were categorized by their authors as odes, or were written in open emulation of approved Classical models. The very rare exceptions have been poems which are universally regarded as belonging to the genre.

5
Some Twentieth-Century Odes

Perhaps the word 'ode' seems to promise a magniloquence to which few twentieth-century writers have aspired. At all events, they have been notably reluctant to incorporate it in the titles of their poems. Early in the century, Robert Bridges (1844–1930), Lascelles Abercrombie (1881–1938), and Laurence Binyon (1869–1943) used it in connection with works that now arouse little interest. The finest poem of the century to be so designated by its author is probably the 'Ode to the Confederate Dead' of Allen Tate (born 1899).

As a Southerner, Tate feels a kinship with those killed in the struggle against the Federal armies. An earlier Southerner, Henry Timrod (1828–67), wrote immediately after the American Civil War an 'Ode Sung on the Occasion of Decorating the Graves of the Confederate Dead, at Magnolia Cemetery, Charleston, S.C., 1867'. This begins:

> Sleep sweetly in your humble graves,
>   Sleep, martyrs of a fallen cause;
> Though yet no marble column craves
>   The pilgrim here to pause.
>
> In seeds of laurel in the earth
>   The blossom of your fame is blown,
> And somewhere, waiting for its birth,
>   The shaft is in the stone!

Though Tate's ode is much longer than Timrod's, his words seem to come less easily. He records the autumnal desolation of the cemetery:

Row after row with strict impunity
The headstones yield their names to the element,
The wind whirrs without recollection;
In the riven troughs the splayed leaves
Pile up, of nature the casual sacrament
To the seasonal eternity of death;
Then driven by the fierce scrutiny
Of heaven to their election in the vast breath,
They sough the rumour of mortality.

When he has invoked the Conferate dead, what is the poet to say?

Now that the salt of their blood
Stiffens the saltier oblivion of the sea,
Seals the malignant purity of the flood,
What shall we who count our days and bow
Our heads with a commemorial woe
In the ribboned coats of grim felicity,
What shall we say of the bones, unclean,
Whose verdurous anonymity will grow?
The ragged arms, the ragged heads and eyes
Lost in these acres of the insane green?
The gray lean spiders come, they come and go;
In a tangle of willows without light
The singular screech-owl's tight
Invisible lyric seeds the mind
With the furious murmur of their chivalry.

We shall say only the leaves
Flying, plunge and expire.

The poet's reserve accentuates his grief; his regret makes itself felt more strongly through his detachment.

In an 'Ode' written during the nineteen-thirties, Louis MacNeice (1907–63) characteristically declares his acceptance of necessary limitation:

I do not want a hundred wives or lives
Any more than I want to be too well-read
Or have money like the sand or ability like the hydra's heads

> To flicker the tongues of self-engendering power,
> I want a sufficient sample, the exact and framed
> Balance of definite masses, the islanded hour;

and he utters a corresponding prayer for his child:

> I would pray off from my son the love of that infinite
> Which is too greedy and too obvious; let his Absolute
> Like any four-walled house be put up decently.

He does not employ even the muted rhetoric of Allen Tate; he writes easily, casually, apparently refusing to take his art too seriously.

Sadly, almost fatalistically, as in his other writings of the period, he acknowledges the imminence of war. His contemporary, W. H. Auden (born 1907), expresses likewise an awareness of an inevitable commitment to conflict in various poems published early in the same decade. The one starting, 'Though aware of our rank and alert to obey orders', appeared originally as 'Ode', later received the title, 'Which Side Am I Supposed to Be On?' and later still became 'Ode' again. The speaker's side preserves distinctions of rank, upholds military discipline, and receives the Church's blessing; the opposing side consists of the deprived and the excluded. Auden presents the struggle between them with a teasing ambiguity. Is the war a real war, or a boys' adventure-story war? Is the conflict social, or psychological, or both at once? Does the business call for a grim, or a jocular, presentation? There are times when we have to doubt which side we are supposed to be on. Nevertheless, our first glimpse of the rebels determines our general attitude for the rest of the poem:

> Now we're due to parade on the square in front of the Cathedral,
> When the bishop has blessed us, to file in after the choirboys,
> To stand with the wine-dark conquerors in the roped-off pews,
>   Shout ourselves hoarse:
> 'They ran like hares; we have broken them up like firewood;
>   They fought against God'.

While in a great rift in the limestone miles away
At the same hour they gather, tethering their horses beside them;
A scarecrow prophet from a boulder foresees our judgment,
    Their oppressors howling;
And the bitter psalm is caught by the gale from the rocks:
    'How long shall they flourish?'

What have we all been doing to have made from Fear
That laconic war-bitten captain addressing them now?
'Heart and head shall be keener, mood the more
    As our might lessens':
To have caused their shout 'We will fight till we lie down beside
    The Lord we have loved'.

The contrast between the two congregations, together with the tellingly placed quotation from the Anglo–Saxon *Battle of Maldon* in the middle of the third stanza quoted, successfully enlists our support for the outcasts.

Auden again refuses to be too much in earnest when, a couple of decades later, he addresses the earth, 'our Mother, the/nicest daughter of Chaos', in an affectionate, mocking 'Ode to Gaea'. Only the self-denying ordinance formulated at the end of Chapter 4 prevents me from bringing into our account a number of poems which Auden does not call odes. 'A Summer Night', for example, is surely an Horatian echo; and the 'Anthem for St Cecilia's Day', written for Benjamin Britten, could claim consideration along with Dryden's great odes for music. But such an extension of the accepted terms of reference would admit much more than a few poems by Auden. If MacNeice's 'Ode' can take the form of a prayer for his son, why should not 'A Prayer for my Daughter' of W. B. Yeats (1865–1939) be thought an ode? And would it not be reasonable to include Yeats's 'Easter 1916' along with Marvell's great 'Horatian Ode'? And did not Dylan Thomas (1914–53) produce several examples without affixing the label?

It seems clear that modern poets fight shy of calling an ode an ode. No doubt they fear that the title promises too much. They do not wish to commit themselves to being as weighty and as dignified as their readers will expect the composers of odes to be. Moreover, they share with these readers some uncertainty regarding the advisability of classifying unique works of literature in genres.

As we have seen, these hesitations are of relatively recent growth. To the Elizabethans, an ode could be a short, light song. In the seventeenth and eighteenth centuries, the greater ode established itself in imitation of Pindar, the lesser ode in imitation of Horace. These Classical influences became more diffuse during the Romantic period. Many of our finest odes, both formal and irregular, appeared during the early years of the nineteenth century and imparted an impulse that persisted throughout the Victorian age. But during this age authors began to use the title 'ode' less readily, until in our own century it has been widely abandoned as an embarrassment.

This being its history in England, can we give any single sense to the word 'ode'? Clearly we cannot. But we can say that in the nineteenth and twentieth centuries the word has been used to refer to lyrical poems which, originating in personal impulses, rise to the presentation of general ideas of some gravity and substance. Most of these poems are of moderate length and are fairly elaborate in structure and in style. Many of them take the form of addresses, though this is now less common than it was when the Classical influence was more potent. Poems which possess some but not all of these attributes may still be acceptably termed odes.

If anyone should object that this description leaves as much uncertainty as did that quoted from the *Oxford Dictionary* in Chapter 1, my reply must be that the objection, though justified, is not really very damaging. Any rigid definition would impose an arbitrary order on recalcitrant material. In the end the only acceptable way of defining the ode is by discussing numerous indubitable instances. This is what I have tried to do.

Select Bibliography

A. *Texts*

For the convenience of readers who do not have easy access to large libraries, I have as far as possible used as my examples poems contained in *The New Oxford Book of English Verse 1250–1950* (ed. Helen Gardner, Oxford, 1972). At the same time, I have preferred to take my quotations from texts which follow the original spelling and punctuation of the poems more closely than would have been appropriate in the *New Oxford Book*.

Necessarily, many of my examples come from outside the limits of Helen Gardner's anthology. Full texts of some of them are readily available in the collected editions by which major writers are represented in such series as the Oxford Standard Authors. But a number of my examples are by writers who have not yet been honoured in this way. Many of these can be found in the Oxford Books devoted to particular areas. *The Oxford Book of Seventeenth Century Verse* (ed. H. J. C. Grierson and G. Bullough, Oxford, 1934) contains the poems that I have mentioned by DRAYTON, BEN JONSON, HERBERT, RANDOLPH, FANSHAWE, and MARVELL, as well as COWLEY's ode beginning 'This only grant me'. *The Oxford Book of Eighteenth Century Verse* (ed. D. Nichol Smith, Oxford, 1926) contains the poems by WATTS, COLLINS, and GRAY from which I have quoted. *The Oxford Book of American Verse* (ed. F. O. Matthiessen, New York, 1950) contains the poems by TIMROD and TATE. Poems included neither in these anthologies nor in the various well-known series of collected editions may be traced through the following list, which points also to recommended translations of Pindar and Horace:

AUDEN, W. H., *Collected Shorter Poems 1927–1957*, London, 1966.

BINYON, R. LAURENCE, *Collected Poems*, 2 vols, London, 1943.

CONGREVE, WILLIAM, *Complete Works*, ed. M. Summers, 4 vols, London, 1923.

COWLEY, ABRAHAM, *Poems*, ed. A. R. Waller, Cambridge, 1905. Contains Cowley's Pindaric odes.

DRAYTON, MICHAEL, *Minor Poems*, ed. Cyril Brett, Oxford, 1907.
Includes all the odes.

HOPKINS, GERARD MANLEY, *Poems*, fourth edition, ed. W. H. Gardner and N. H. Mackenzie, London, 1967.

HORACE, *Odes*, trans. James Michie, London, 1964.
Translations into English verse are printed opposite to the Latin texts.

LANDOR, WALTER SAVAGE, *Poetical Works*, ed. S. Wheeler, 3 vols, Oxford, 1937.

MACNEICE, LOUIS, *Collected Poems*, ed. E. R. Dodds, London, 1966.

PATMORE, COVENTRY, *Poems*, ed. F. Page, London, 1949.

PINDAR, *Odes*, trans. C. M. Bowra, Penguin Classics, Harmondsworth, 1969.
Free-verse translations of the odes arranged in a likely chronological order, with compact Introduction and useful notes.

PRIOR, MATTHEW, *Literary Works*, ed. H. B. Wright and M. K. Spears, 2 vols, second edition, Oxford, 1971.

SURREY, HENRY HOWARD, EARL OF, *Poems*, ed. Emrys Jones, Oxford, 1964.

SWINBURNE, ALGERNON CHARLES, *Complete Works*, ed. E. Gosse and T. J. Wise, 20 vols, London, 1925–7.

THOMAS, DYLAN, *Collected Poems 1934–1952*, London, 1952.

YEATS, W. B., *Collected Poems*, second edition, London, 1950.

B. *Historical and Critical Studies*

BOWRA, C. M., *Greek Lyric Poetry from Alcman to Simonides*, Oxford, 1936.
Substantial essays on Alcman, Stesichorus, Alcaeus, Sappho, Ibycus, Anacreon, and Simonides.

BOWRA, C. M., *Pindar*, Oxford, 1964.
An exhaustive critical study, covering Pindar's theory of poetry; his religious, political, and athletic ideals; the structure, imagery, and style of his odes; his treatment of myth; and his poetical personality.

GOAD, C., *Horace in the English Literature of the Eighteenth Century*, New Haven, 1918.
A useful reference-book, consisting mainly of a vast appendix cataloguing allusions to Horace in the works of fourteen writers. Prior and Pope are among these, but the author thinks Addison 'the most truly Horatian writer of the eighteenth century' (p. 15).

HEATH-STUBBS, JOHN, *The Ode*, London, 1969.
A discursive introduction, illustrated by copious quotation. Twenty-five poems are given in their entirety. Could be regarded as an anthology of Classical and English odes with a helpful running commentary.

HIGHET, GILBERT, *The Classical Tradition: Greek and Roman Influences on Western Literature*, Oxford, 1949.
Chapter 12, 'The Renaissance and Afterwards: Lyric Poetry', is largely concerned with the Pindaric and Horatian traditions.

HOPKINS, KENNETH, *The Poets Laureate*, London, 1954.
A popular account of the poets who have held the Laureateship since the post was instituted in the seventeenth century. The appended selections from their works include a number of passages from their official odes.

LEISHMAN, J. B., *Translating Horace: Thirty Odes translated into the original metres with the Latin Text and an Introductory and Critical Essay*, Oxford, 1956.
The long and comprehensive introductory essay includes a straightforward account of Horace's metres.

MADDISON, CAROL, *Apollo and the Nine: A History of the Ode*, London, 1960.
A thoroughgoing account of the ode in European literature from Pindar, Anacreon, and Horace to the latter part of the seventeenth century. The author gives special attention to the Renaissance writers of odes in Latin, who 'invented a new poetic genre, a poem celebrating contemporary experience in the ancient taste' (p. 2). In her longest chapter, on the English ode, she calls Drayton 'the first proper ode writer in English' (p. 295), describes Milton's 'Nativity Ode' as 'the greatest ode in the English language' (p. 321), and credits Cowley with creating 'a new English poetic form, the formal lyric, on a serious subject or a significant occasion, studied, grandiose, and magniloquent, yet brightly decorated, lively, and enthusiastic' (p. 400).

SHAFER, ROBERT, *The English Ode to 1660*, Princeton, 1918.
Thoroughgoing and informative, but sometimes rather narrowly prescriptive.

SHUSTER, GEORGE N., *The English Ode from Milton to Keats*, New York, 1940.
A comprehensive survey, in which attention is paid to the relationships between poetry and music.

THAYER, M. R., *The Influence of Horace on the Chief English Poets of the Nineteenth Century*, New Haven, 1916.
Consists mainly of lists of allusions to Horace in the works of seven major poets. Useful for reference.

WILLIAMS, GORDON, *The Nature of Roman Poetry*, Oxford, 1970.
An abbreviated and simplified version of the same author's *Tradition and Originality in Roman Poetry*, Oxford, 1968. Catullus, Propertius, Virgil, and Horace are the poets who receive the closest attention.

Index